O THE NEW WORLD

P9-DZM-627

PORTUGAL   SPAIN

PALOS

SANTA MARIA   CANARY
ISLANDS

GOMERA
DAY 1   GRAND
CANARA

AFRICA

E A N V S

N T A L I S

Indian

INDIAN RIVER AREA LIBRARY
3 8610 00002898 2

INDIAN R

I, Columbus

My Journal ~ 1492-3

I, Columbus

My Journal ~ 1492-3

Edited by
Peter and Connie Roop

Illustrated by
Peter E. Hanson

WALKER AND COMPANY
NEW YORK

Indian River Area Library
P.O. BOX 160
INDIAN RIVER, MICHIGAN 49749

Copyright © 1990 by Peter and Connie Roop
Illustrations © 1990 by Peter E. Hanson
All rights reserved. No part of this book may be reproduced or
transmitted in any form or by any means, electronic or mechanical,
incuding photocopying, recording, or by any information storage and
retrieval system, without permission in writing from the Publisher.

First published in the United States of America in 1990
by Walker Publishing Company, Inc.

Published simultaneously in Canada by Thomas Allen & Son
Canada, Limited, Markham, Ontario

Library of Congress Cataloging-in-Publication Data

I. Columbus / edited by Peter and Connie Roop :
illustrated by Peter E. Hanson.
Summary: Follows the voyages of discovery made by Christopher
Columbus through excerpts from the journals he kept of his travels.
ISBN 0-8027-6977-2.—ISBN 0-8027-6978-0 (lib. bdg.)
1. Columbus, Christopher—Diaries—Juvenile literature.
2. Explorers—America—Diaries—Juvenile literature. 3. Explorers—
Spain—Diaries—Juvenile literature. 4. America—Discovery and
exploration—Spanish—Juvenile literature. [1. Columbus,
Christopher—Diaries. 2. Explorers—Diaries. 3. America—Discovery
and exploration—Spanish. 4. Diaries.] I. Roop, Peter. II. Roop,
Connie. III. Hanson, Peter E. ill.
E118.I2   1990
970.01′5—dc20   [92]   90-12407

Printed in Hong Kong

2   4   6   8   10   9   7   5   3   1

Book Design by Shelli Rosen

Excerpted, with permission, from book #60660 Log Of Columbus, by Robert K. Fuson.
Copyright 1987 by Robert K. Fuson. Published by International Marine/TAB BOOKS, a division
of McGraw-Hill, Blue Ridge Summit, PA 17294.

*For Scott O'Dell and Elizabeth Hall
whose insights into life, now and long ago,
continue to inspire us.*

Prologue

Columbus was the finest sailor of his time. He knew the winds and the waters. He knew his locations from the sun and the stars. Watching a log float from bow to stern he could calculate how fast his ship sailed. He had sailed south along the coast of Africa, navigated north to England and Iceland, criss-crossed the Mediterranean Sea, and sailed west to the Canary islands. "I went to sea at an early age," he wrote in 1501. "There I have continued to this day. I have sailed everywhere that it is navigable."

Christopher Columbus had a dream. He would sail west to reach the fabled lands of the East, rich in spices, jewels, silver, and gold—especially gold. The mysteries and wealth of India, Japan, and China called to him from halfway around the world. Columbus knew other explorers had reached the Indies by traveling east over land and sea. He had read their books, marked their maps, studied their charts. His own notes and ideas filled the margins of his copy of Marco Polo's *Travels*.

Columbus convinced Queen Isabella and King Ferdinand that they could capture Jerusalem with the gold he brought back from the Indies. "I have already petitioned Your Highnesses that all of the profits of my enterprise should be spent on the conquest of Jerusalem. Your Highnesses smiled and said this idea pleased them," Columbus wrote in his Log.

So it was that on August 3, 1492, Christopher Columbus and eighty-nine men set sail on a voyage to the unknown. This Log is Columbus's record of that voyage, told in his own words.

I, Columbus

My Journal ~ 1492-3

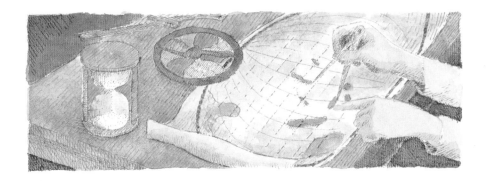

Most Christian, exalted, excellent, and powerful Princes, King and Queen of the Spains and of the islands of the seas, our Sovereigns; It was in this year of 1492 that Your Highnesses concluded the war with the Moors who reigned in Europe. In the same month, based on the information that I had given Your Highnesses about the land of India and about a Prince who is called the Great Khan, which in our language means "King of Kings," Your Highnesses decide to send me, Christopher Columbus, to the regions of India, to see the Princes there and the peoples and the lands, and to learn of their disposition, and of everything, and the measures which could be taken for their conversion to our Holy Faith.

In May of 1492 I went to the town of Palos, which is a seaport. There I fitted out three vessels, very suited to such an undertaking. I left Palos well supplied with a large quantity of provisions and with many seamen on the third day of the month of August. I set my course for the Canary Islands of Your Highnesses, which are in the Ocean Sea, from there to embark on a voyage which will last until I arrive in the Indies and do all that Your Highnesses have commanded me to do.

To this end, I, Columbus, decided to write down everything I might do, see, and experience on this voyage, from day to day, and very carefully. I intend to draw a chart of all of the seas and lands in the Ocean, in their true places and with their correct bearings. Moreover, I will compose a book and illustrate everything in true picture. Above all, it is fitting I should forget about my sleep and pay great attention to my navigation. These things will be a great task.

Indian River Area Library
P.O. BOX 160
INDIAN RIVER, MICHIGAN 49749

~ August ~

Friday, 3 August 1492. We set sail at eight o'clock in the morning. The wind is strong and variable. We had gone forty-five miles by sunset. After dark I changed course for the Canary Islands.

Monday, 6 August, 1492. The rudder of the *Pinta* slipped its socket. The heavy sea prevented me from helping, but I was able to come alongside the *Pinta* and hearten the crew. Despite the trouble we were able to make eighty-seven miles last night and today.

Wednesday, 8 August, 1492. I decided to go to Grand Canary Island and leave *Pinta* for she was badly disabled and leaking.

Thursday, 9 August, 1492. The *Pinta* was able to reach Grand Canary this morning. I ordered Martin Pinzon, the captain, to remain until the *Pinta* could be properly repaired. I took the *Santa Maria* and the *Nina,* and set out for the island of Gomera. If I cannot find another vessel there, I will come back in a few days and help with repairs.

Friday, 17 August, 1492. Two weeks have passed since our departure, and the crew has become restive.

Saturday, 18 August, 1492. I went ashore at Gomera to see if another ship might be available, but none of the few crafts is capable of a voyage of any length over the open sea. I must accept those things I cannot control. My enterprise is in God's hands.

Thursday, 23 August, 1492. It is essential that we sail west soon.

Friday, 24 August, 1492. At daybreak I weighed anchors. I passed the night near Tenerife where the great volcano on that island erupted in a fiery display. Many members of the crew were frightened, for they had never seen such an event. I calmed them by telling about other volcanoes I have seen, and explained the cause of this great fire.

Saturday, 25 August, 1492. I reached Grand Canary this morning. Martin Pinzon had not repaired the rudder, a fact that disturbs me. I am determined to make a new rudder for the *Pinta*.

~ September ~

Monday, 3 September, 1492. Guiterrez has already acquired all of the wood and water necessary for the voyage, which I estimate will last twenty-one days. However, to be on the safe side, in case of contrary winds or currents, I ordered Guiterrez to prepare for a voyage of twenty-eight days. I anticipate no problem in replenishing our supplies when we reach the Indies.

Tuesday, 4 September, 1492. Today we loaded and stored dried meat and salted fish, and some fruits. The fruit will be consumed early, for it will spoil if the voyage is of three weeks' duration.

Wednesday, 5 September, 1492. All is ready for the voyage. Tonight I shall order a special service of thanksgiving; at sunrise I will lift anchors to begin the journey westward.

Thursday, 6 September, 1492. Shortly before noon I sailed and set my course for the west. I sailed all day and night with very little wind.

Sunday, 9 September, 1492. This day we completely lost sight of land. Many men sighed and wept for fear they would not see it again for a long time. I comforted them with great promises of lands and riches. I decided to count fewer miles than we actually made. I did this so the sailors might not think themselves as far from Spain as they really were. For myself I kept a confidential, accurate, reckoning. Tonight I made ninety miles.

Monday, 10 September, 1492. Today I made one hundred eighty miles. I recorded only one hundred forty-four miles in order not to alarm the sailors.

Saturday, 15 September, 1492. I sailed west day and night for eighty-one miles. Early this morning I saw a marvelous meteorite fall into the sea twelve or fifteen miles away. Some people took this to be a bad omen, but I calmed them by telling them of the numerous times that I have seen such events. I have to confess that this is the closest a falling star has ever come to my ship.

Monday, 17 September, 1492. I held my course to the west and made one hundred fifty miles, but I logged only one hundred forty-one miles. I saw a great deal of weed today from rocks that lie to the west. I take this to mean that we are near land. The crew found a live crab in a

patch of it. This is a sure sign of land. Everyone is cheerful. The *Pinta,* the fastest sailing vessel, went ahead in order to sight land. We saw a lot of porpoises, and the men of the *Nina* killed one with a harpoon. All the indications of land come from the west, where I trust Almighty God, will soon deliver us to land.

Tuesday, 18 September, 1492. I sailed day and night for one hundred sixty-five miles, but I recorded only one hundred forty-four miles. Martin Pinzon, who sailed ahead yesterday lay-to waiting for me. He hoped to sight land last night; that is why he was going so fast. He is a fine captain and very resourceful, but his independence disturbs me. I trust that this striking out on his own does not continue, for we can ill afford to become separated this far from home. He tells me that at sundown he saw land about forty-five miles to the north. My calculations indicate land is not in that direction. I am not going to waste time with it.

Thursday, 20 September, 1492. Today I changed course for the first time since departing Gomera. Early this morning three little birds flew over the ship, singing as they went. This was a comforting thought, for unlike the large water birds, these little birds could not have come from far off.

We saw much weed stretching to the north as far as you can see. This weed comforted the men, since they concluded that it must have come from some nearby land. At the same time, it caused great apprehension because in places it was so thick it held back the ships. The men

thought the weed might become so thick that we might become stuck as did St. Amador when a frozen sea held his ship fast. We kept as clear as possible from those weed mats.

Friday, 21 September, 1492. Today was mostly calm. By night and day I made about thirty-nine miles. The sea is as smooth as a river. I saw a whale, another sign of land, for whales always stay near the coast.

Sunday, 23 September, 1492. The crew is grumbling about the wind. The changing wind, along with the flat sea, has led the men to believe we will never get home. I told them being near land keeps the sea smooth. Later, when waves arose without wind, they were astonished. I saw this as a sign from God. Soon the wind arose and the sea grew rougher. The crew was relieved. The men tried to catch fish but could not get any to bite at the hooks. Eventually they harpooned several.

Monday, 24 September, 1492. I am having serious trouble with the crew, despite the signs of land that we have.

All day long and all night long those who get together never stop complaining. They fear they will not return home. They have said that it is insanity and suicidal to risk their lives. They say I am willing to risk my life to become a great Lord and that I have deceived them to further my ambition. I am told by a few trusted men (and these are few in number!) that if I persist in going onward, that the best course of action will be to throw me into the sea some night. They will say I fell overboard while taking the position of the North Star.

I know the men are taking these complaints to Pinzon. I know he cannot be trusted. He is a skilled mariner, but he wants the rewards and honors of this enterprise for himself. He is always running ahead of the fleet, seeking to be the first to sight land.

Tuesday, 25 September, 1492. At sunset Pinzon called to me that he saw land and claimed the reward. I fell to my knees to give thanks to Our Lord. The *Nina*'s crew all climbed the mast and rigging, and claimed that it was land. I myself was sure it was land about seventy-five miles to the southwest.

Wednesday, 26 September, 1492. After sunrise I realized that what we all thought was land was nothing more than squall clouds, which often resemble land. I returned to my original course of west in the afternoon, once I was positive I had not seen land. Day and night I sailed ninety-three miles, but recorded seventy-two. The sea was like a river and the air sweet and balmy.

Saturday, 29 September, 1492. I sailed on to the west, making seventy-two miles by day and night, but told the crew sixty-three miles. I saw many flying fish. They are about a foot long and have two little wings like a bat. These fish fly above the water and sometimes they fall on our ships. The sea is as smooth as a river, and the breeze is delightful and pleasing.

~ October ~

Monday, 1 October, 1492. I sailed west for seventy-five miles but reckoned sixty. It rained very hard this morning. The pilot of the *Santa Maria* calculated that we had gone 1,734 miles; I gave him my corrected figure of 1,752. My personal calculation shows we have come 2,121 miles. I did not reveal this to the men because they would become frightened, finding themselves so far from home, or at least thinking they were that far.

Thursday, 4 October, 1492. I sailed west, between day and night making one hundred eighty-nine miles. More than forty petrels came to the ship at one time, along with two terns. A boy on the *Pinta* hit one with a stone. So many birds are a sure sign that we are near land.

Saturday, 6 October, 1492. I maintained my course to the west. This evening Pinzon told me it would be wise to steer southwest by west to reach the island of Japan. In my opinion it is better to continue directly west until we reach the mainland. Later we can go to the islands on the return voyage to Spain. My goal is the Indies, and it would make no sense to waste time with offshore islands. My decision

has not pleased the men. Despite their grumblings I held fast to the west.

Sunday, 7 October, 1492. This morning we saw what appeared to be land to the west, but it was not very distinct. No one wished to make a false claim of discovery.

However, this morning at sunrise the *Nina* ran ahead, fired a cannon, and ran up a flag on her mast to show land had been sighted. Joy turned to dismay as the day progressed for by evening we had found no land and had to face the reality that it was only an illusion.

Wednesday, 10 October, 1492. Between day and night I made one hundred seventy-seven miles. I told the crew one hundred thirty-two miles, but they could stand it no longer. They grumbled and complained of the long voyage. I told them that, for better or worse, they had to complete the voyage. I cheered them on, telling them of the honors and rewards they would receive. I told them it was useless to complain. I had started to find the Indies and would continue until I had.

Thursday, 11 October, 1492. I sailed to the west-southwest. The crew of the *Pinta* spotted reeds and a small board. A stick was found that looks man-made, perhaps carved with an iron tool. These made the crew breathe easier; in fact, the men have even become cheerful. A special thanksgiving was offered to God for giving us renewed hope through the many signs of land.

About ten o'clock at night I saw a light to the west. It looked like a wax candle bobbing up and down. It had the same appearance as a light or torch belonging to fishermen or travellers who raised and lowered it. I am the first to admit I was so eager to find land that I did not trust my own senses so I called Gutierrez and asked him to watch for the light. After a few moments, he too saw it. I then summoned Rodrigo Sanchez. He saw nothing, nor did any other member of the crew. It was such an uncertain thing I did not feel it was adequate proof of land. Then, at two hours after midnight, the *Pinta* fired a cannon, my signal for the sighting of land.

I now believe the light I saw was truly land. When we caught up with the *Pinta,* I learned Rodrigo de Triana, a seaman, was the first man to sight land. I lay-to till daylight. The land is about six miles to the west.

Friday, 12 October, 1492. At dawn we saw naked people. I went ashore in the ship's boat, armed, followed by Martin Pinzon, captain of the *Pinta,* and his brother Vincente Pinzon, captain of the *Nina.* I unfurled the royal banner and the captains brought the flags. After a prayer of

thanksgiving, I ordered the captains to witness I was taking possession of this island for the King and Queen. To this island I gave the name San Salvador, in honor of our Blessed Lord. No sooner had we finished taking possession of the island than people came to the beach.

The people call this island Guanahani. Their speech is very fluent, although I do not understand any of it. They are a friendly people who bear no arms except for small spears. They have no iron. I showed one my sword, and through ignorance he grabbed it by the blade and cut himself.

I want the natives to develop a friendly attitude toward us because I know they are a people who can be converted to our Holy Faith more by love than by force. I think they can easily be made Christians, for they seem to have no religion. I will take six of them to Your Highnesses when I depart, in order that they may learn our language.

I gave some red caps to some and glass beads to others. They took great pleasure in this and became so friendly it was a marvel. They traded and gave everything they had with good will, but it seems to me that they have very little and are poor in everything. I warned my men to take

Indian River Area Library
P.O. BOX 160
INDIAN RIVER, MICHIGAN 49749

nothing from the people without giving something in exchange.

This afternoon the people came swimming to our ships and in boats made from one log. They brought parrots, balls of cotton thread, spears, and many other things. We swapped them little glass beads and hawks' bells.

Saturday, 13 October, 1492. I have tried very hard to find out if there is gold here. I have seen a few natives wear a little piece of gold hanging from a hole made in the nose. By signs, if I interpret them correctly, I learned by going south I can find a king who possesses great containers of gold. I tried to find some natives to take me, but none want to make the journey.

This island is large and very flat. It is green, with many trees. There is a very large lagoon in the middle of the island. There are no mountains. It is a pleasure to gaze upon this place because it is all so green, and the weather is delightful.

In order not to lose time I want to set sail to see if I can find Japan.

Sunday, 14 October, 1492. I made sail and saw so many islands that I could not decide where to go first. The men I captured indicated there were so many islands they could not be counted. I looked for the largest island and decided to go there.

Wednesday, 17 October, 1492. I named this island Fernandina. There are many things that I will probably never know because I cannot stay long enough to see everything. I must move on to discover other islands and to find gold.

All the people I have seen so far resemble each other. They have the same language and customs.

All of the trees are as different from ours as day is from night, and so are the fruits, the herbage, the rocks, everything. The fish are so unlike ours that it is amazing; some are like dorados, of the brightest colors in the world—blue, yellow, red, multi-colored, colored in a thousand ways; the colors so bright that anyone would marvel and take great delight at seeing them. Also, there are whales. I have seen no land animals except parrots and lizards. I have not seen sheep, goats, or any other beasts.

Friday, 19 October, 1492. I simply do not know where to go next. I never tire from looking at such luxurious vegetation. I believe there are many plants and trees here that would be worth a lot in Spain for use as dyes, spices, and medicines, but to my great sorrow I do not recognize them. You smell the flowers as you approach this coast; it is the most fragrant thing on earth. Before I depart, I am going ashore to explore.

Sunday, 21 October, 1492. At ten o'clock in the morning we anchored. Flocks of parrots darken the sun. Birds of so many species so different from our own that it is a wonder. I am bringing a sample of everything I can. I saw a serpent, which we killed with lances. I am bringing Your Highnesses the skin. The people here eat them. The meat is white and tastes like chicken.

Sunday, 28 October, 1492. At sunrise I approached the coast of Cuba. I am now certain that Cuba is the Indian name for Japan. I have never seen anything so beautiful. The country is full of trees. I took a small boat ashore and approached two houses. The people fled in fear. We found a dog that did not bark. We found nets and cords made of palm threads, fishhooks made of horn, harpoons made from bone. I ordered not one thing be touched. The Indians say on this island there are mines of gold and pearls. I saw a good place for the pearls. I was given to understand large ships belonging to the Great Khan came here. From the mainland it is 10 days journey. I must try to go to the Great Khan, for he is in the city of Cathay. This is a very great city, according to what I was told before leaving Spain.

~ November ~

Saturday, 3 November, 1492. Many canoes came to the ships to trade things made of spun cotton, including the nets in which these people sleep, called hammocks.

Monday, 5 November, 1492. At dawn I ordered the *Nina* beached in order to clean the hull. I shall do the *Pinta* next and then the *Santa Maria*. Two ships should remain in service all the time for security reasons, although here people are safe and I could beach all three ships together without fear. This is one of the best harbors in the world, and it has the best climate and the friendliest people.

Thursday, 8 November, 1492. Our work on the ships is not complete and the winds are still contrary. I therefore have postponed my departure, and will remain here until the ships are ready.

Sunday, 11 November, 1492. It would be well to take some of these people, in order that they might learn our language and we might learn what there is in this country. Upon return, they may speak the language of Christians and take our customs and Faith to their people. Today there came to the ship a canoe with six youths in it, and five came aboard. These I ordered held and am bringing them with me. I sent men to a house west of the river, and they brought seven women and three children. Tonight the husband of one of the women, and father of the children, came to the ship. He asked that I might let him come with us. It pleased me greatly. All the people on board are now consoled.

Wednesday, 21 November, 1492. This day Martin Pinzon sailed away with the *Pinta,* without my will or command. It was through treachery. I think he believes that an Indian I placed on the *Pinta* could lead him to much gold, so he departed without waiting and without the excuse of bad weather, but because he wished to do so.

Thursday, 22 November, 1492. Last night after Pinzon sailed away I could see him for a long time, until he was twelve miles away. That night was very clear and the light wind favorable for him to sail in my direction if he had chosen to do.

Friday, 23 November, 1492. I sailed all this day toward the land to the south. Visible in the distance is another land or cape that extends to the east. The Indians aboard call this Bohio, and say it is very large and has people with one eye in the forehead as well as others they call cannibals of whom they show great fear. When they saw I was taking that course, they were too afraid to talk. They say that the cannibals eat people and are well armed. The Indians we have met believed the same thing at first about us Christians.

Sunday, 25 November, 1492. I saw a large stream of very fine water, which fell from a mountain and made a great noise. I went to the river and saw in it some stones, glittering like gold. I ordered certain stones gathered for the Sovereigns. The ships' boys cried out they saw pines. I cannot exaggerate their height and straightness like spindles. I knew ships could be made from these, and there is a great quantity of timber and masts for the largest vessels of Spain.

I cannot express to you, my Sovereigns, what a joy and pleasure it is to see all this. I have not praised it a hundredth part of what it deserves, and it pleases our Lord to continually show me something better, for always in what I have discovered up to the present it has gone from good to better, in trees, forests, grasses, fruits, flowers, and in the people. The same is true about the harbors and waters. When one who has seen all of this wonders at it so greatly, how much more wonderful will it be to those who merely hear of it. No one will be able to believe all of this until he sees it.

∼ December ∼

Wednesday, 5 December, 1492. I have decided to leave Cuba which up to now I thought to be the mainland. I have

sailed along its coast three hundred sixty miles. I will sail
to Bohio which lies southeast. It is a very great island say
the Indians who are very afraid of the inhabitants of Bohio.
They believe those of Bohio eat people.

Thursday, 6 December, 1492. At dawn I found myself twelve
miles from land. At the hour of vespers we entered a
harbor I named in honor of St. Nicholas because it was his
feast day. I marveled at the beauty and excellence of this
harbor. We shall call this land Isla Espanola.

Monday, 17 December, 1492. I sent men to a village and by
trading some worthless glass beads they obtained gold
beaten into the form of a thin leaf. I saw one man they call
Cacique, whom I take to be the governor of the province.

Tuesday, 18 December, 1492. I remained anchored today
because there is no wind. More than two hundred men
came with the Cacique and four men carried him on a
litter. The Cacique arrived while I was eating. He saw I was
eating and came quickly to seat himself beside me, but
would not allow me to rise or interrupt my meal. After the

meal a servant brought a belt. He gave this to me, along with two very thin pieces of gold. I saw the cover on my bed pleased him, so I presented it to him, along with some amber beads that I wore around my neck. I also gave him some red shoes and a flask of orange water. This pleased him wonderfully. I also showed him the royal banners which he admired greatly. He told his men that Your Highnesses must be great Lords, since you sent me here so far without fear. Many other things were said that I did not understand, except I saw everything was wonderful.

Friday, 21 December, 1492. Today I saw a harbor on Isla Espanola which surpasses any other. I have been sailing for twenty-three years and have seen all the East and West and have traveled through Guinea, but in all those regions harbors as perfect as these will never be found. I have considered what I, have written very carefully, and I assert I have written correctly and now this harbor surpasses all the others. All the ships in the world could be contained in it.

Indian River Area Library
P.O. BOX 160
INDIAN RIVER, MICHIGAN 49749

The people here have no spears, arrows, or other arms. I ordered that at no time were any of my men to annoy any of these people in any manner and that no one was to take anything from them against their will. I cannot believe that we have found a people with such good hearts, so liberal in giving, and so timid, that they strip themselves of everything to give all they have to us.

Sunday, 23 December, 1492. I sent two Indians to villages. They returned to the ships with a Chief and with the news that in this Isla Espanola there is as much gold as we desire. In the three days I have been in this harbor I have received good pieces of gold. May Our Lord, Who has all things in His hands, assist me and direct me in finding the gold.

I think that more than one thousand persons came to the ship, all bringing something. Even before these canoes reached the ships, the Indians arose and held up what they were bringing saying, "Take, take." I think another five hundred swam because they did not have canoes, and we were anchored three miles from land!

Tuesday, 25 December, 1492—Christmas Day. I sailed in a light wind yesterday. I decided to lie down to sleep because I had not slept for two days and one night. Since it was calm, the sailor who was steering the ship also decided to catch a few winks and left the steering to a young ship's boy, a thing I have always expressly prohibited throughout the voyage. It made no difference whether there was wind or calm; the ships were not to be steered by young boys.

The currents carried the ship upon a bank so quietly that it was hardly noticeable. When the boy felt the rudder ground and heard the noise of the sea, he cried out. I jumped up instantly; no one else had yet felt that we were aground. I ordered the master of the ship to rouse the crew, to launch the small boat and to take the anchor and cast it at the stern. I assumed they were following my orders. Instead, their only thoughts were to escape to the

Nina. The crew of the *Nina* would not receive them which was correct.

I ordered the mast cut and the ship lightened as much as possible, to see if it could be refloated. But the water became even more shallow, the ship settled more and more to one side. I could not save her.

I took my crew to the *Nina* for safety. I dispatched the master-at-arms to go directly to the King and to beg him to come to this harbor with his boats. My men told me that the King wept when he heard of the disaster. He sent all his people from the village with many large canoes to help us unload the ship. Everything was unloaded in a very brief space of time. The King personally assisted in the unloading and guarded whatever was taken ashore. I certify to Your Highnesses that in no part of Castile could things be so secure. Not even a shoe string was lost!

Wednesday, 26 December, 1492. At sunrise the King came to the *Nina,* where I was, and almost in tears told me not to be dismayed because he would give me whatever he had.

I ordered a lombard and a musket be fired. The King was spellbound when he saw the effect of their force.

When the people heard the shots, they fell to their knees. They brought me a large mask, which had pieces of gold in the ears and eyes. The King placed this, along with other jewels of gold, on my head and around my neck. I derived great pleasure and consolation from these things. I realized this eased the trouble and affliction I had experienced by losing the ship. I recognized that Our Lord had caused me to run aground at this place so that I might establish a settlement here.

Now I have ordered a tower and a fortress be built. It is necessary for the Indians to know what we can do, in order that they may obey Your Highnesses with love and fear.

Monday, 31 December, 1492. Today I saw that water and wood were taken aboard for the departure for Spain. I would like to see all the land along this coast, but I have only one ship remaining. It does not appear reasonable to expose myself to the dangers that might occur in making anymore discoveries. All this trouble and inconvenience has arisen because the *Pinta* deserted me.

~ January ~

Wednesday, 2 January, 1493. I left on Isla Espanola thirty-nine men in the fortress. I have left with them all the

merchandise purchased for trading. With this they may trade for gold.

I charged the three officers to see that everything was well ruled and governed for the service of God and Your Highnesses.

Friday, 4 January, 1493. At sunrise I weighed anchors in a light wind. I sailed east toward a very high mountain.

Sunday, 6 January, 1493. After midday the wind blew strongly from the east, and I ordered a sailor to climb to the top of the mast to look out for shoals. He saw the *Pinta* approaching and she came up.

Martin Alonso Pinzon came aboard the *Nina* to apologize, saying that he had become separated against his will. He gave many reasons for his departure, but they were all false. I do not know why he has been so disloyal and untrustworthy toward me on this voyage.

The *Pinta's* crew had traded for a great deal of gold. Pinzon took half and divided the other half among his people. So, Lords and Princes, I know Our Lord miraculously ordered the *Santa Maria* should remain here because it is the best place on all the islands to make a settlement, and it is near the gold mines.

Tuesday, 8 January, 1493. I have decided to return with the greatest possible haste and not stop any longer. Although there are many disobedient people among the crew, there are also many good men.

Wednesday, 16 January, 1493. Three hours before dawn I departed.

Wednesday, 23 January, 1493. Last night there were many changes in the wind. I waited many times for the *Pinta* which had difficulty sailing close to the wind because the mast was not sound. The sky is very disturbed these days, but it has not rained and the sea is very calm all the time, many thanks given to God.

Friday, 25 January, 1493. The sailors killed a porpoise and a very large shark. These were necessary because we had nothing to eat except bread, wine, and ajes from the Indies.

~ February ~

Tuesday, 12 February, 1493. I sailed to the east during the night and by sunrise had made a distance of fifty-four

miles. I began to experience heavy seas and stormy weather. If the ship had not been very sound and well equipped, I fear we would have been lost. During the day I made thirty-six miles with great difficulty and in constant danger.

Wednesday, 13 February, 1493. From sunset until sunrise I experienced great difficulty with the wind, high waves, and a stormy sea. There has been lightning three times, which is a sure sign of a great storm coming. I went with bare masts most of the night, then raised a little sail and went about thirty-nine miles. The sea became terrible, with the waves crossing each other and pounding the ships.

Thursday, 14 February, 1493. The wind increased last night and the waves were frightful, coming in opposite directions. They crossed each other and trapped the ship, which could not go forward nor get out from between them, and they broke over us. Seeing the great danger I began to run before the wind, letting it carry me wherever it wanted, for there was no other remedy. The *Pinta* also began to run and eventually disappeared from sight, although all night I showed lights and the *Pinta* responded until it was not able to do so any longer because of the force of the storm.

The great desire I have to bring this wonderful news to Your Highnesses causes me to fear I will not succeed in doing so. It seems to me than even a gnat can disturb and impede it. I attribute this to my little faith and lack of confidence in the Divine Providence. On the other hand, I am comforted by the favors God has bestowed upon me by giving me such a victory in discovering what I have discovered. I believe that God will fulfill what has begun and that He will deliver me safely. This is especially so since He delivered me from the difficulties I had at the outset of the voyage when the sailors with one voice determined to return and rebel against me. Therefore, I ought not to fear this storm. But my weakness and anxiety will not allow my mind to be reassured.

I also feel great anxiety because of the two sons I have in Cordoba at school, if I leave them orphaned. I am concerned because Your Highnesses do not know the service I have rendered on this voyage and the very important news I am carrying to you. For this reason, I have written on a parchment everything I can concerning what I have found, earnestly beseeching whomsoever might find it to carry it to Your Highnesses. I sealed the parchment in a waxed cloth, tied it very securely, took a large wooden barrel, and placed the parchment in the barrel, without anyone knowing what it was (they all thought it was some act of devotion), and had it thrown into the sea.

Friday, 15 February, 1493. Last night, after sunset, the skies began to clear to the west. The sea is subsiding a little.

After sunrise we saw land. Some said it was Madeira; others the Rock of Sintra in Portugal, near Lisbon. We must be fifteen miles from land. According to my navigation I think we are off the Azores and believe the land ahead is one of those islands. The pilots and sailors believe that we are already off Spain.

Sunday, 17 February, 1493. I rested a little last night because I have not slept since Wednesday, and my legs have become cramped from exposure to the cold and water and from having so little food. At sunset I reached the island, but it was so dark and cloudy I could not recognize what island it was.

Monday, 18 February, 1493. Yesterday after dark I went around the island to see where I could anchor. The men learned that this is the island of *Santa Maria,* one of the Azores. The people here had never seen such a storm as that which has prevailed for fifteen days, and they wondered how we escaped. They offered many thanks to God and rejoiced greatly when they heard the news that we had discovered the Indies.

My navigation has been very accurate, and I have steered well. I was sure we were in the vicinity of the Azores. I pretended to have gone a longer distance to confound the pilots and sailors who steered, and to remain master of the route to the Indies, because none of them is certain of my course and none can be sure of my route to the Indies.

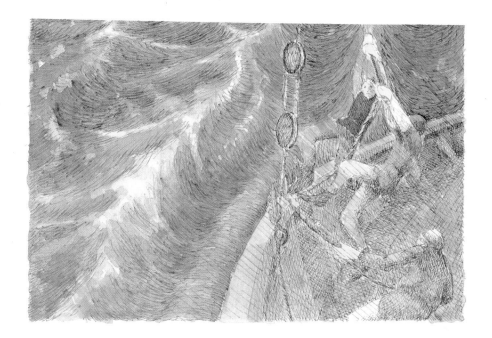

Thursday, 21 February, 1493. I am astonished at such bad weather as there is in these islands. In the Indies I sailed all winter without anchoring because of the weather which was good all the time. The sacred theologians and learned philosophers were quite correct when they said the earthly Paradise is at the end of the Orient, because it is a most temperate place. Those lands I have now discovered are at the end of the Orient.

Monday, 25 February, 1493. Last night I sailed to the east, on course, the sea calm, thanks be to God. A very large bird, an eagle, came to the ship.

Wednesday, 27 February, 1493. I am very concerned with storms, now that I am so near the end of my journey.

~ March ~

Monday, 4 March, 1493. Last night we experienced a terrible storm and thought we would be lost because the waves came from two directions, and the wind appeared to raise the ship in the air, with the water from the sky and the lightning from every direction. It pleased Our Lord to sustain us, and we continued in this fashion until the first watch, when our Lord showed us land. God protected us until daylight, but it was with infinite labor and fright.

When the sun came up I recognized the land which was the Rock of Sintra, near the river at Lisbon. I decided to enter because I could not do anything else. I learned from the seafaring people that there never has been a winter with so many storms; twenty-five ships had been lost.

I wrote the King of Portugal, who was twenty-seven miles from here to ask permission to land at Lisbon.

Tuesday, 5 March, 1493. Bartolome of Diaz of Lisbon, master of the large ship of the King of Portugal, better equipped with cannons and arms than any ship I have ever seen, came to the *Nina* with an armed vessel. He told me to get aboard his ship to give an account of myself to the King.

I replied, "I am the Admiral of the Sovereigns of Castile. I will not leave my ship unless compelled to do so by force of arms."

He replied, "Send the master of your ship."

I said, "I will send neither the master nor any other person unless by force because I consider it the same to allow another person to go as myself. It is the custom of Admirals of the Sovereigns of Castile to die rather than send their people."

He changed his demands and said that since I had made that determination, it should be as I wished, but he requested to see the letters from Your Highnesses, if I had them. It pleased me to show them to him. He returned to his ship and told his Captain who then came to the *Nina* with great ceremony, complete with trumpets, pipes, making a great display.

Wednesday, 6 March, 1493. When word spread I had come from the Indies, many people came to see me and the Indians. It was wonderful to see the way they marveled at us.

Saturday, 9 March, 1493. The King himself received me with great honor and showed me much respect, asking me to sit down and talking very freely with me.

Monday, 11 March, 1493. Today I took leave of the King.

Friday, 15 March, 1493. I continued my course until dawn with a light wind. I entered the bar at Sales until I was inside the harbor from which I had departed on August 3 of the past year. Thus, the writing is now completed. I intend to go by sea to Barcelona where, Your Highnesses are staying. This is in order to give a full account of my voyage, which Our Lord has permitted me to make. This voyage has proven to be a miraculous voyage despite the opposition of so many principal persons of your household, who were all against me and treated this undertaking as a folly. I hope to Our Lord that it will be the greatest honor for Christianity, although it has been accomplished with such ease.

Your servant,
Christopher Columbus, Lord Admiral of the Ocean Sea.

Indian River Area Library
P.O. BOX 160
INDIAN RIVER, MICHIGAN 49749

Epilogue

Columbus presented this Log to Queen Isabella and King Ferdinand in April, 1493. The Queen immediately ordered a scribe to make an exact copy for Columbus, now Admiral of the Ocean Sea. Columbus received the copy just before he sailed on his second voyage in September. This version of the Log is based upon that copy. The original Log disappeared soon after Isabella's death in 1504.

Columbus journeyed to the New World four times. On each voyage he encountered new adventures and endured new hardships. On each voyage he believed he had reached the Indies. Christopher Columbus died in 1506 never knowing he had discovered a new world.

Acknowledgements

Robert H. Fuson translated this version of Christopher Columbus's log. It was published as *The Log of Christopher Columbus* by Maine International Marine Publishing Co., Camden, Maine, in 1987. Mr. Fuson, an avid sailor, retraced Columbus's first voyage following the Log, measuring the miles, and seeing the same sights that Columbus saw five hundred years ago. We owe a debt of great appreciation to Mr. Fuson. His fascination with Columbus, his knowledge of Spanish, and his understanding of sailing, allowed us to join Columbus on his great adventure.

Most of all we express our awe of Columbus himself, a man with a vision and the determination to accomplish it.

COLUMBUS'S

NORTH
AMERICA

NINA

COLUMBUS

COAT OF ARMS

ISLAND NAMES
TODAY

WATLING
ISLAND

LONG
ISLAND

SAMANA CAY
DAY 33

RAGGED
ISLAND
RANGE

CROOKED

ACKLINS
ISLAND

FORTUNE
ISLAND

GREAT INAGUA
BABEQUE

CUBA

PINTA

PINTA

ILE DE LA   WRECK
TORTUE   SANTA MARIA

PUERTO
RICO

HISPANIOLA
HAITI   DOMINICAN
REPUBLIC

A   T

O

JAMAICA

SOUTH
AMERICA